MY INTIMATE
RELATIONSHIP WITH GOD

Through Poetry

Written By: Sandra Dawn Swaby Robinson

Book Design & Editing: Aaron C. Butler

Written By: Sandra Dawn Swaby Robinson
Book Design & Editing: Aaron C. Butler

© 2024 BookButler Publishing Company

ISBN 9798988696186 (Paperback)
ISBN 9798988696193 (eBook)

Printed in the United States of America

BookButler Publishing Company
Upper Marlboro, MD 20774

TheBookButler.com

BookButler Publishing Company titles may be purchased in bulk for educational, business, fundraising, or sales promotional use. For information, please email: info@ thebookbutler.com

Dedication

This book of spiritual poems is dedicated to the three most
important men in my life.
First to my Lord and Savior who guides and protects my life,
I will forever honor your unconditional love for me and put no
one above you. Thank you, Lord, for the words of wisdom.
Secondly, to my son, Omar. It's my joy and pleasure to be
your mother. You captured my heart from the day you were
born. I love you with every beat of my heart.
Thirdly, to my husband, Ransford. You taught me the
meaning of true love and communication. You help me
to serve God in a deeper way.

Acknowledgment

No man stands alone, and in my quest to publish my first book, I would like to acknowledge the following people who made the journey easier for me:

Graemme Denyce Boone – My sister-in-Christ, thank you for your encouraging words and for introducing me to my publisher, Aaron Butler, and the BookButler Publishing Team.

Mitchell Robinson – My niece, thank you for teaching me how to use my laptop and for proofreading my work.

Dr. Janice Parks – My sister-in-Christ, thank you for your willingness to proofread my poems. Your advice was invaluable and easy to apply.

Kereisha Taylor – My Goddaughter, thank you for constantly reminding me to complete this book. Your care and love mean the world to me.

Introduction

Poetry for me is the best way I know how to express my joys and sorrows. My mother used to sit with me around the dining table most evenings encouraging me while I write about anything and everything.

Around fourteen years ago I surrendered my heart to the Lord, today I'm still working to maintain my faith in him.

LORD…..

I am nervous, feeling so afraid
My life's about to change, in a spiritual way
I'm reaching out to you, my Savior
Finally! in an intimate way
Where do I start? What do I say?
Lord, I want to be worthy of your love
I need you, Lord; I need you today

I am so emotionally lost, so insecure
I need you Lord now, for sure
I'm like an empty barrel rolling around
Sometimes I'm up; sometimes I'm down
So here I come Lord, baggage and all
A sinner searching, please, answer my call

"My Heavenly Father……………

Table of Contents

A Prayer Today

Lord, I kneel down to you and pray
Please wash my sins and troubles away
Take control of my health and weakness
Please take away all my sickness

Lord, as I pray
Watch over my family and friends today
Let's all learn to care for each other
Love one another like sisters and brothers

Lord, I pray for my community
Show us how to live in unity
Love our neighbors as our friends
Pour blessing on all of them

Lord, the world we all living in, needs your blessing here
Global wars, violence, and hatred are everywhere
I pray for the wars and rumors of wars to cease
And let all the countries in the world find some sense of peace

Lord, as I kneel down to you and pray
Please hear my prayer today
I know it's a lot I'm asking you to do
But you say, bring all problems to you

Lord, I give you all the glory
Lord, I give you all the praise
Till you call me home at the end of my day
I'll love and worship you always
This is my prayer for today

"Talking to the Lord you can't go wrong.
A prayer always keeps your faith strong."

Before I Slept

A prayer made before I slept last night
Oh Lord, my life just isn't right
I'm heading down the road of destruction
Reach out to me Lord; give me some direction

A prayer made before I slept last night
A few family passed, now out of my sight
They died and left me year after year
Is this my year I wonder? Living daily in fear

A prayer made before I slept last night
Take the world out of the darkness, into the light
Wars and violence all over; people living in sorrow
Being evil and acting like there's no tomorrow

A prayer made before I slept last night
What can I do to make it right?
Showing all love and respect
Help and give the needy each chance I get

I know we can make this world a better place
Love each other regardless of culture, religion, and race
Ask the Lord daily for guidance to live by
That's the prayer made before I slept last night

"Pray each night before you sleep.
You'll sleep peacefully while God watches and keeps."

Blessing On Me

Thank you, Lord, for your blessing on me
Even when I'm not worthy of your love
Thank you, Lord, for your blessing on me

Lord, my heart is willing, why my mind so weak
I seek your guidance each day of the week
Trying to understand your desire of me
And what you require my life to be

Lord, I get angry when I should rejoice
Blaming human behavior for my negative choice
It's hard at times to live by your way
But I'll keep on trying to be better each day

Lord, I need to be deserving of your love
You give so abundantly from above
Even when I mess up and sin
On you I call, and you cleanse me within

Mom lectures your words to me all day long
So, I know the difference between right and wrong
Though temptation often leads me astray
Lord by my side, you always stay

Thank you, Lord, for your blessing on me
Even when I'm not worthy of your love
Thank you, Lord, for your blessing on me

"Seek God; He is waiting with Grace and Mercy.
He showers us with all his blessings."

Sandra Dawn Swaby Robinson

Call Me Home

You are my stronghold in times of trouble
In you, I depend on and never worry
You are the beginning and the end
My life is in your hands until you say when

No more Lord will I roam
On that day when you call me home
Oh, your glorious face Lord I'll see
In Heaven's gate; my final destiny

"Heaven's gate is in sight at the end of your days.
If you live your life the Lord's way."

Call On You

Woke up feeling a bit lifeless
Focus on financial pressure and crisis
Forgetting for a moment I'm not alone
Nor needing to call someone on the phone
I'll call the one who's flawless and fearless
My one and only Savior Jesus

Jesus, I call on you
To guide and see me through
You are my strength and anchor
You are my blessed Savior
With you Jesus, I'm favored

With all my discretion, you wipe me clean
Grant me forgiveness and set me free
With you Jesus, I'll never roam
From my faith in you, I've come to know
Glad you're right here by my side
Your spiritual comfort makes me alright

"Jesus is our one and only Savior.
With Him, we are truly favored."

Couldn't See

Lord, you are wonderful, wonderful to me
When I lost all my loved ones
Hatred I carry for Thee
Though you didn't love me
Lord, I couldn't see
Your reason for doing things
Didn't affect your love for me
Lord, you are wonderful, wonderful to me
Been to death door more than once
Though that was it for me
When the doctor says fifty-fifty
Lord, one hundred percent you guarantee me
Lord, I couldn't see
You're the one that rescued me
Lord, you are wonderful, wonderful to me

You, I try to understand and know
To see if your direction I should go
Learn about your unfailing love
You give so abundantly from above
Now I understand and see
Now I'm worshipping and serving only Thee
Lord, you are wonderful, wonderful to me
Once weak, blind, and couldn't see
Today my faith is strong
My soul is now at ease
How wonderful is my Lord
The one who first and forever loves me
Lord, you are wonderful, wonderful to me

"Don't be spiritually blind; seek Jesus now."

Faith

My faith Lord is so strong within me
In you Lord I do believe
Need my faith to take me all the way
To Heaven's gate on that blessed day

Faith in God, Oh I do believe
Trust in Him and you shall receive
If you don't believe a word I say
Just look at me today
An unbeliever in the past
Now worshipping and praising God at last

I learn the values of faith
And about God who I come to appreciate
My heart now is at ease
God took my burden and gave me peace
With joy, He fills my soul
And with his blessing, I will be made whole

My faith Lord is so strong within me
In you Lord I do believe
Need my faith to take me all the way
To Heaven's gate on that blessed day

"Faith is total loyalty to God.
With the assurance of believing what we cannot see."

Guide Me Lord

I lift my hand and praise you, Lord
I give you my heart from now to start
You take my sins and wash them away
Constantly guiding me each and every day

Around me Lord, people live in doubt
Have no idea what you're all about
Their faith and knowledge are nil about you
I know that feeling; I've been there too

You stand by me and give me strength
I take my troubles to you Lord, and vent
Sometimes life pressure makes me cry
And often times Lord, I will ask you why

The failures in life that come my way
Makes me a better person here today
Through the rough roads, I climb to be free
I want to thank you, Lord, for guiding me

I lift my hands and praise you, Lord
I give you my heart now from the start
You take my sins and wash them away
Constantly guiding me each and every day

Ask for guidance and it shall be given.
In the Bible, it is written."

Heart Wide Open

I'm here now Lord
My heart wide open to you
I need your strength now Lord
To daily carry me through

Going through life hopelessly
Living without you
Then you step in, saying it's time my child
Lord, in your direction I now pursue

You're the foundation today in my life
The source of all good things that's right
Everything I want and need to live
Is available, Lord, by grace and faith you give

Thanks for what you're doing for me
Future hopes and blessings to see
Lord, you never broke a promise to me
In my joys and sorrows, always there for me

I'm here now, Lord
My heart wide open to you
I need your strength now, Lord
To daily carry me through

"Give a testimony of what God's done for you.
So, others can seek Him too."

Honor You

You know me, Lord
All my inside and out
And despite all my flaws
You still love me, Lord

I live my life
With all its ups and downs
Through all the joys and pain
I honor and give praise to Your name

The devil tries to take control
He is determined to win my soul
But I stood steadfast in my faith
Wanting to be worthy of your loving grace

I will honor and worship You
To Your name, Lord I'll be true
I will put no one above You
My faith in you will carry me through
Until that day when I'm face to face with You

You know me, Lord
All my inside and out
And despite all my flaws
You still love me, Lord

"Honor God only.
Cause only He is worthy."

Hope

Lord, renovate my heart, make it pure
Strengthen my faith, make it more secure
Give me the guidance each day to do
What is required according to you

I need Your blessing for today
I need it more than yesterday
When things go wrong and I can't cope
I need your blessing, Lord, to give me hope

Build me a spiritual foundation to stand
I don't want to slip and slide in quicksand
Lord, lead me down the road to righteousness
Rid me of my fear, faults, and weaknesses

I need your blessing for today
I need it more than yesterday
When things go wrong and I can't cope
I need your blessing, Lord, to give me hope

"When all is lost and you're at the end of the rope.
Seek and surrender to God; He'll help you cope."

I Call

Lord, you are my rock and fortress
My deliverer when I'm in distress
I pour my heart out to you
For God, you are my refuge

I call to you Lord
You're worthy to be praise
I give you all the glory
And honor to your name

I medicate on your rules
And consider your ways
I will obey your words
For the rest of my days

Show me your unfailing love oh Lord
Your salvation you grant to me
Direct me in the path of your command
And set my heart free

I call to you Lord
You're worthy to be praise
I give you all the glory
And honor to your name

"Call on the Lord anytime.
He'll answer your call in His given time."

I'm Glad Lord

I seek you, Lord and you answer me
Great advice and guidance you give to me
I put my trust and faith in you
Lord, only you can carry me through

Lord, I'm glad you're around
You keep my feet on solid ground
You are my strength and shield
My heart and soul, Lord, you heal

Like a blind man, I couldn't see
The unconditional love you have for me
Like a mute, I couldn't speak
To shout out all the blessings you give to me

Good things come to those who pray
So, I call on you, Lord, every day
My prayer you answer in your time Lord
So, I patiently await my reward

Lord, I'm glad you're around
You keep my feet on solid ground
You are my strength and shield
My heart and soul, Lord, you heal

"Surrender to God is not that bad.
Just worship Him only; guarantee you'll be glad."

I'm Here Lord

I'm here, Lord
I love you more each day
I'm here, Lord
Don't let me go astray
I'm here, Lord
Guide and protect me always
I'm here Lord
With you, forever I'll stay

I feel your presence within me
A steady inner joy shining brightly
You enlighten me, Lord, showing me the way to go
Terminate my worries, fears, and sorrows

Everything I need Lord,
It's within reach by faith and grace
I call on you, and you're always ready to embrace
Polish my endeavors and use them to your will
Serving you constantly, I will never stand still

I commit myself totally to you
Guide and help me, Lord, to keep my faith with you
I'm at ease now; I have you with me
I plant you in my heart, where you'll forever be

"Talk to God each day.
He's not tired to hear you say...
Lord I'm here, I love you always."

Just for Me

Lord, you are my stronghold in times of trouble
My deliverer from the wicked and evil
At times my sins overpower me, I cannot see
Thank you, God, for rescuing me

Just for me, just for me
You bear all my pain and burden
Just for me
Just for me, just for me
Your son you send to die on Calvary
Just for me
Just for me, just for me
For me, you have done things marvelously
Just for me, Lord, just for me

You hear my prayer when I call on you
You deliver my needs on your timetable
You build the land, air, and sea
The mountain, hill, and valley for me

Your unfailing love you grant to me
I fully embrace wholeheartedly
You are my refuge and my shield
My love and faith in you; I sealed

Just for me, just for me
You bear all my pain and burden
Just for me
Your son you sent to die on Calvary
For me, you have done things marvelously
Just for me, Lord, just for me

"Jesus shed His blood for us all.
His hands and feet bear the scars; just for me."

Knowing My God

Lately, I'm getting to know this man above
Finding you now; so easy to love
Learning about you really opens my eyes
I'm grateful to you Lord! for sparing my life

A lot of things about God I don't know
And why you love a sinner like me so
Reading the Bible, trying to understand the scriptures
What does it mean for me

He gave His only son to die for me
So, I can live and be totally sin-free
Being ignorant, I took Him out of my thoughts
Knowing him now! He'll never leave my heart

He wants me to love my neighbor as my friend
Live and obey all His commandments
Show love and kindness to all mankind
And He'll honor my needs; but in His time

This man called God, a jealous one He says
Wants me to love and worship Him only each day
With my renewed faith and love for my God
I'm going to worship Him with all I got

"To know God
Is to serve and love God."

Life Journey

My faith in you Lord
So strong now in me
As I face the rough challenges
Life has in store for me

Through life's journey, I bear major pain
An emotional agony at times, drives me insane
The devil rejoices when I'm in this stage
But God, my defender; you keep me safe

Living by your words Lord every day
I'm your servant here, guide me the right way
Let me understand the goals you set out for me
And in the direction, you want my life to be

Through life's journey, I bear much lost
But thinking back on what Jesus did for me on that cross
For my life, my sins, and all my negative faults
I will forever pray, honor, and sing praises
In your name my Lord

My faith in you Lord
So strong now in me
As I face the rough challenges
Life has to offer me

"Walk with God every day.
Live your life always the righteous way."

Lord Is

Lord is the ruler of this earth
In Him, I put first
There's no one above Him
He's Lord Almighty, my King
Lord is my only Savior
In me He favors
I give my heart to Him forever
Knowing He'll leave me never
Lord is my defender
From evil forces who try to devour
My shield and my protector
Lord, you rule forever and ever
Lord is my strength
On Him, I can always depend

When I'm down and in doubt
I call on Him, He sought me out
Lord is kind and loving
Love me so unconditionally
Even when I'm not deserving
To me, He keeps on giving
Lord is waiting on you
Seek Him now, see what He can do
Get to know what He's about
Give Him a chance; check Him out

"He's our protector and deliverer.
Our one and only Lord and Savior."

Lord, I Thank You

Live my life being the boss of me
Though I made it solely independently
Forgot the man who shed His blood for me
Lord, I thank you

Woke up this morning feeling brand new
Lord, I thank you
Opened the blind, the sun shining through
Lord, I thank you
Beautiful weather to start the day too
Lord, I thank you
I give you the glory and the praise
Lord, I thank you
Thank you in advance for today
Yes, Lord, I thank you

Though I had it all till I found you
Without you Lord my life has no value
You taught me the true meaning of life's worth
Lord, you are the King of this earth
Lord, I thank you

"Whether good or bad; thank the Lord each day.
He wakes you up each morning; consider today a great day."

Love You Lord

What you do for me Lord I can't repay
I just have to honor and serve you each day
I thank you for the breath I take
Each morning as I wake

CHORUS: I love you Lord
You do so much for me
I love you, Lord
I smile brightly for all to see
I love you, Lord
You're in control of my life
I love you, Lord
My walk, talk, destiny, and all

I want the world to see
How you make me feel
My heart is bursting with joy
From the day you rescued me

I lift my hands in praise to you
I honor and put no one above you
No more Lord will I roam
Serving you only till you call me home

CHORUS

"The word of God is contagious.
So spread the words of His love for all of us."

My Heart

My heart now says yes Lord
Want you to be the one I cling to
My heart now says yes Lord
Want to love you more than I used to
My heart now says yes Lord
Want to lift my hands in praise to you
My heart now says yes Lord
Want to sing out loud and glorify you
My heart now says yes Lord

Once down and emotionally distressed
Though you abandoned me and didn't care less
Though I'll deal with it alone
Without you, God, and fix it on my own

Something happens to me one day
You stepped into my path God and led me your way
Had my blindfold on. Couldn't see what you were about
That by my side you stood, during my downs and outs

Today I put you in full control
Of my mind, body, and soul
Use me Lord to your will
My heart says yes Lord
Your desire of me, I will fulfill

"God is the only way.
Let Him in your heart today."

My Life

I search my heart and soul out deeply
Found it in need of renovation quickly
My foundation is weak and thin
To fix it Lord, I'll have to let you in

You plan out my life for me
And the way it ought to be
I wasn't living that life your way
I'm changing my direction, gladly today

Lord, it's a privilege to know you
It's an honor to be loved by you
A love you give so willing and easily
Lord, I love you

I'm now trying to live my life right
I'm out of the darkness, aiming for the light
No more Lord, will I roam
I'm your servant Lord; use me till you call me home

Free and happy forever
Oh, what a day that will be
My life, I'll do my best to live it righteously
For your face Lord, I want to see

What a day that will be
When I'm face to face with you, Lord Almighty
And to see your face smiling down on me
Saying, "Welcome Child! Welcome home to me"

"Live your life right.
Keep God in your sight.
When earth life ends; eternal life begins."

My Lifeline

Every rough hill I climb
Lord, you're my protector, my lifeline
So many dark days you see me through
I love you, Lord, I really do

With all my ups and downs
My ins and outs
Lord, you took full control of me
When I slip and fall
And fight to get up
You're there ready to rescue me

You are my Savior
You mean everything to me
Without you Lord, I'm nothing
Without you, I'm totally empty

With all my ups and downs
My ins and outs
Lord, you took full control of me
When I slip and fall
And fight to get up
You're there ready to rescue me

"God knows our ins and outs.
Seek Him first, He will rescue and seek you out."

My Provider

When I think of all the good things you have done for me
The positive way my life turns out to be
I know you are with me all the way
I feel your undying love for me always

Lord, you are my strength and protector
My provider and my keeper
I put no one above you
Oh Lord, I love and adore you

Such a blessing to know you care
I just call out your name and Lord, you're there
You encircle me with love and grace
Not even the devil can rock my faith

I wake each morning and give you praise
I spread your word of love and your amazing grace
I want everyone who doesn't know you like I do
To know what it is like to seek and worship you

I live my life right in honor of you
I steer my life in the direction you lead me to
Knowing at the end of my days, I'll see your face
When you welcome me through Heaven's gate

Lord, you are my strength and protector
My provider and my keeper
I put no one above you
Oh Lord, I love and adore you

"For all the rough hills you'll climb.
The Lord, our protector, is our lifeline."

Sandra Dawn Swaby Robinson

No One Like You Lord

Thank you, Lord, for your blessing on me
Blessings, you pour so constantly
Lord, there is no one like you
Who loves me wholeheartedly, the way you do

Lord, I ask for forgiveness each day
You turn and wash my sins away
Daily I ask for strength and protection too
You're right there Lord, ready to rescue
Traveling mercies, you send my way
I love you, Lord, more each day

The devil tries to block my path
But his temptation never lasts
He tries to take control of me
But Lord, your mighty power is greater than he

When I'm drowning in sorrow, I do not fear
I know you Lord, you're always near
You wipe my tears and comfort me
"I'm here for you child," you whisper to me
A sinner like me! And you love me so
I'm hungry now for your love, Lord
I'll never let you go

Thank you, Lord, for your blessing on me
Blessings, you pour so constantly
Lord, there is no one like you
Who loves me wholeheartedly the way you do

"Our Lord is one of a kind; He's Lord Almighty
He loves each and every one of us unconditionally."

Not Happy

I thought my life was paste with gold
Enjoying all good things life could hold
When issues arrive, I take it in stride
Financially secure to survive

I open my Bible today and read
Finding out, without God, my life is totally incomplete
I need to make that change today
And put God in front of everything I do and say

Without you Lord I'm not happy
I want you in my life today
Without you Lord I'm not happy
I want you in my heart to stay
Without you Lord I'm not happy
I surrender my all to you today
Without you Lord I'm not happy
Until I honor and give all praises to you
Without you Lord I'm not happy
Cause happiness is knowing I've got you

"Be happy to know our God.
Happiness is knowing in your heart that you God."

Only You

I'll leave it all to you Lord
Cause only you can see me through
My faith in you is all I need
I'll follow you Lord as you lead

I'll pay attention to your words of wisdom
Lord, I'll heel to your words
Along the straight path you lead me
I will not stumble as I go

I won't forget your teaching
Your commands are stored in my heart
I acknowledge you Lord in every way
Love and faithfulness to you, I'll never stray

I'll leave it all to you Lord
Cause only you can see me through
My faith in you is all I need
I'll follow you Lord as you lead

"Your faith will carry you through
Serve only Him, it's all He asks of you."

Possibilities

Been hiding from you Lord so long
Living the life, I know is wrong
Today I change and make it right
Giving you my heart, Lord, without a fight

The possibilities
Lord, you offer to me
Just change my way of life
Now I'm living righteously
Your undying love you give to me
Is more than I deserve
But I accept willingly
I'll do my best Lord not to displease
To earn your trust, to gain all possibilities

Lord, you are my strength and deliverer
My protector and anchor
When I'm down and drowning in sorrow
You guide me to the light, to a brighter tomorrow

I love you, Lord
More and more each day
I worship you, Lord
In every possible way
My heart I give only to you
My soul, faith, and trust belong to you, too

"In life, there is no guarantee.
With God in your life, you'll reap all the glory and possibilities."

Praising You Lord

Lord, I adore you in so many ways
I lift up my hands in praise to you every day
For years I omit you from my thoughts
But you, Lord, were always in my heart

All the pains and burdens I bear
I thought you never really care
All the angry words I yell at you
You stand by me still and guide me through

So many nights I cry myself to sleep
When I should ask you, Lord, for my soul to keep
I blocked you out when you took the family I had
Still, you love me, my forgiving God

Lord, I'm ready for you to use me now
And if I'm in doubt, please show me how
I know your presence is here with me
Cause you take my pain away and set me free

Lord, I adore you in so many ways
I'll keep praising you, for the rest of my days
I will sing and dance praises in your name
I now accept you in my heart Lord, always

"Never give up on God.
He'll never give up on you."

Surrender

I'm going to get to know you, Lord
Going to live my life right
Some commandments seem hard to do
But my faith in you, hope to carry them through

I'm going to serve you, Lord
Put my total trust in you
You're now a constant force in my life
Morning, noon, and night

I'm going to surrender to you
I'm going to give you all of me
Going to show you how strong my love can be
Want to be deserving of your love given to me

I'm going to put no one above you
Going to worship only you
Lord, you're my rock and foundation
My creator over all nations

I want to walk through Heaven's gate
When my life here on earth is through
Lord, I want to run into your welcome arms
Having eternal life with you

"Surrendering your heart. So easy to do.
The Lord is patiently waiting on you."

Take Control

I trust you, Lord, without hesitating
My loyalty to you so genuine
My faith in you keeps me so secure
I'll lift my hand to you, Lord my Savior

Lord, take control of me
I've tried it alone and failed miserably
Take control of me
I need you now Lord, desperately
Take control of me
Without you Lord, I'm empty
Take control of me
Use me your way, Lord, I'm ready

Your words Lord are right and true
You're faithful in all that you do
Even when I slip and stray a bit
Your undying love for me; you never quit

You're my strength and my refuge
My salvation depends solely on you
You have my heart and my soul
I'll follow your lead, Lord, please take control

Lord, take control of me
I've tried it alone and failed miserably
Take control of me, Lord
Use me your way, Lord! I'm ready

"Have God in control in all you do.
At the end, Heaven's gate will be open for you."

Thank You, Lord

Thank you, Lord, for good and bad times
The smooth and rough hills I climb
Thank you, Lord, for my life today
For showering me with blessings always

Through pain and sorrow
The hardship of life I'd swallow
The good times and life great rewards
I raise my hands to you; thank you, Lord

You stand by me when no one can
Embrace me when I fall with your mighty hand
When I'm at fault, and when I sin
You cleanse me, Lord, deep within

Feeling down and insecure
Wondering what my future has in store
Lord, will my life be better today
Or a future of continuous replay

Woke up this morning, the sun shining through
What's in store for me today? I have no clue
Lord, you prepare a menu for my life
And with my faith in you, I will apply

Thank you, Lord, for good and bad times
The smooth and rough hills I climb
Thank you, Lord, for my life today
For showering me with blessings always
Thank you, Lord

"Thank the Lord for everything.
Regardless of the situation you are in."

To Be Worthy

He saves me from all my sins
Even when I'm not deserving
He shows me unfailing love
Love I know I'm not worthy of
By my side, He'll always be
And knowing He'll never give up on me

I want to be worthy of your love
Want to be worthy of your grace
Lord, you're so good and loving to me
Your precious love I want to be worthy

A place you've gone to prepare for me
So, I can have eternal life with Thee
I'm seeking your Kingdom as you say
Knowing with you, all will be well
My faith grows stronger each day
And pleasing you Lord is the only way

I want to be worthy of your love
Want to be worthy of your grace
Lord, you're so good and loving to me
Your precious love I want to be worthy

"Seek eternal life with Thee.
Have faith knowing that you are worthy."

Trouble Time

To release this pain and hurt I bear
In times of trouble
Oh Lord, I need you near
To release this pain and hurt I bear

Pain burns so deep inside of me
The anger in my heart beats vigorously
You say take my problems to you, Lord, and leave them there
And in your time, you'll answer my prayer

In times of trouble
Oh Lord, I need you near
To release this pain and hurt I bear

At times I find my faith in doubt
Strong emotions drain my self-control out
I'll smile for the world to see
When I'm alone, I'll weep like a baby

Patience is one of my strongest virtues
Allow me to control problems and issues
Even when the devil tries to control me
I look to you, Lord, and you set me free

Lord, you're my guard and protector
Guarding my heart and mind forever
Lord, I'll put my total trust in you
And faith knowing you'll pull me through

In times of trouble, oh Lord, I know you're near

"In times of trouble, the Lord is the only way.
Put your trust in Him today."

Try Jesus

You go around all day
Selling liquor, drug, and weed
Peddling the innocent victim
Up and down the street
Try peddling the words of Jesus
He is the only way
The drugs and weed are temporary
Try Jesus, He's here to stay
You walk the street at night
Selling your body at any price
Degrading your pride and value
Seek Jesus, He will rescue
Try peddling the word of Jesus
He is the only way

Prostituting is temporary
Try Jesus, He's here to stay
Your wealth, money you got plenty
Homeless people living on empty
Share your wealth with the poor
Jesus' blessings will increase galore
Try peddling the word of Jesus
He is the only way
A blessing not be greedy
Try Jesus, He's here to stay

"Try Jesus today. He's able.
To wash and cleanse our sins away. He's capable."

Wake Me

Background blasting with the sound of the alarm
Opening my eyes at the crack of dawn
My vision is slowly focusing
Another day Lord, so glad to be in
Thank you, Lord, for another day to see
All the possibilities you have in store for me
What a beautiful day it's going to be
Negative or positive I'll welcome gladly

Never been this grateful to you each day
Thought it was my luck when I saw another day
I kept you out of my heart and mind all day long
Never reach out, when my days gone right or wrong
Lord, you stood by me and made me see
Despite of me, you love me unconditionally

So, thank you Lord for blessing me
Thank you, Lord, for grace and mercies
Your words of love I'll spread continuously
Another day Lord, thank you for waking me

"Give God thanks for waking you each day.
To new hope, dreams, and possibilities coming your way."

Without You Lord

Wake up each morning feeling so empty
Financially secure, and living life abundantly
I always give back, never been greedy
But my soul is wondering, why I can't feel happy

Without you, Lord
My life is empty
I need you Lord in my life
Guiding me daily
Without you, Lord
My life has no value
Thank you, Lord, for the rescue

Hear a voice inside, softly calling my name
Saying, "I give you love! Return to me the same"
Since that day, my whole life changed
I found you, Lord, and happiness I've gained

Without you, Lord
My life is empty
I need you, Lord, in my life
To guide me daily
Without you, Lord
My life has no value
Thank you, Lord, for the rescue

"Without God, I can't firmly stand.
I'll be a wandering sheep on this Island."

Wonderful To Me

Lord, you are wonderful to me
You're my road and my refuge
The love of others cannot complete
With the unconditional love you have for me

When my faith goes weak within me
You're there ready to refurbish me
When I slip and travel in the wrong direction
You intersect, redirect my destination

You hear my voice when I call
Your mighty hands, Lord, lift me up when I fall
You know the anguish of my soul
Waiting patiently, you step in and take control

I acknowledge my sins to you
You wash and cleanse me through
You turn my hatred into love
Rid my anger with blessings from above

Feels so good to trust in you, Lord
With you, failure will never pour
Having you guiding my life each day
Eternal life I hope for on that fine day

"Knowing and trusting in God is a wonderful thing.
He loves us so much; He died for our sins."

Yet You Still

Yet you still, yet you still
Shower me with blessings
And fill my life with good things
Yet you still, yet you still
Remove all of my sins
Lord, you cleanse me within

Lord, you see me at my worst
Yet you still put me first
I turn my heart away from you
Yet you still help me through
I let go of my faith in you
Yet you still come to my rescue

Lord, I don't help my friends and neighbors
Yet you still grant me favors
Rarely take my problems your way
Yet you still save my day
Living my life in total fear
Yet you still have your presence near

Lord, you don't hear my voice in prayers
Yet you still answer my heart
Your way of life I don't follow
Yet you still prepare my tomorrow
I don't give praise to you every day
Yet you still love me in every way

Yet you still, shower me with blessings
Forgive me of my sins; and cleanse me within

"You all are worthy of God's love.
He will forever shower us with His blessings from above."

Your Blessing

Send your blessing down on me
Give me peace and serenity
Without you Lord I have no joy
Everything I touch, I eventually destroy

Send your blessing, Lord, down on me
I need it now so desperately
Send your blessing down on me
I love you, Lord, oh so deeply
Send your blessing down on me
Thank you, Lord, for what you're doing for me

Feeling ache and pain all over
Call out to you Lord, please heal me all over
Feel your spiritual hands lay firmly on me
My ache and pain disappear so quietly

Such a wonderful God you are to me
Available always in my time of need
You're not selfish and give love so unconditionally
Thank you for the blessing you send down to me

"Don't matter if your faith is weak or strong.
The Lord's blessing covers everyone."

About the Author

Sandra Dawn Swaby Robinson, originally from Jamaica, dedicated ten years to teaching in her homeland. She moved to America to nurture her marriage and family, aiming to provide her son with a brighter future. Sandra enjoys dancing, cooking, reading, and socializing. She has a deep affection for her family, especially her nephews and niece.

Despite enduring the loss of all her siblings and close family members in consecutive years, which tested her faith in God, Sandra remains resilient. In 2008, she was diagnosed with stage 3 kidney disease. This hardship led her to express her struggles and connect with God through poetry.

Today, Sandra's faith is growing stronger. As a devoted servant of God, she acknowledges the long journey ahead and believes that with His grace and mercy, she will one day meet Him.